COLONS AND
SEMICOLONS

BY KATE RIGGS
ILLUSTRATED BY RANDALL ENOS

CREATIVE EDUCATION • CREATIVE PAPERBACKS

Published by Creative Education and Creative Paperbacks
P.O. Box 227, Mankato, Minnesota 56002
Creative Education and Creative Paperbacks are
imprints of The Creative Company
www.thecreativecompany.us

Design and production by Liddy Walseth
Art direction by Rita Marshall
Printed in the United States of America

Illustrations by Randall Enos © 2016

Library of Congress Cataloging-in-Publication Data
Riggs, Kate.
Colons and semicolons / by Kate Riggs; illustrated by Randall Enos.
p. cm. – (Punctuate it!)
Includes bibliographical references and index.
Summary: An illustrated guide to the punctuation marks known as colons
and semicolons, including descriptions and examples of how to properly
use them in lists and in relation to independent clauses.
ISBN 978-1-60818-731-7 (hardcover)
ISBN 978-1-62832-327-6 (pbk)
ISBN 978-1-56660-766-7 (eBook)
1. English language—Punctuation. 2. English language—Usage.
3. English language—Clauses.

PE1450.R513 2016
428.2/3—dc23   2016002549

CCSS: L.1.2; L.2.2; L.3.1, 2, 3, 4, 5; L.4. 1, 2, 3, 4; RI.3.1, 2, 7, 8; RI.4.2, 8

First Edition HC 9 8 7 6 5 4 3 2 1
First Edition PBK 9 8 7 6 5 4 3 2 1

TABLE OF CONTENTS

INTRODUCTION

WHAT IS THAT SOUND COMING FROM THE KITCHEN? **IT'S GRANDMA!** SHE IS COOKING SOMETHING SPECIAL; YOU TAKE A CLOSER LOOK. SHE PUT THESE INGREDIENTS IN THE BOWL: **FLOUR, SUGAR, EGGS, COCOA, AND MORE.** IT'S A BIRTHDAY CAKE, JUST FOR YOU!

PIECE
OF
CAKE

Colons and semicolons are like cocoa. You don't need cocoa to make a cake. But you do need it for a chocolate cake! Some **sentences** are just better with a colon or semicolon.

A colon introduces a list. It comes after an independent **clause**. An independent clause has a **subject** and a **verb**. These parts are what make it "independent."

Jack made pizzas for everyone: pepperoni for Maddie, cheese for Adam, and mushroom for Jenny.

There is a test for using a colon correctly. You should be able to

rewrite the sentence without it.

Jack made pepperoni pizza for Maddie, cheese for Adam, and mushroom for Jenny.

Colons introduce more than just lists: they go before an idea or example, too. A colon shows that what follows is connected to what came before. Think of the stacked dots as pointing back *and* forward.

PUNCTUATION PRACTICE:

If you see a colon, check for the independent clause! Which sentence uses a colon correctly?

1. I made cookies: chocolate chip, peanut butter, and oatmeal raisin.

2. The recipe calls for: macaroni, cheddar cheese, milk, and butter.

A: Sentence 1 is correct. "I made cookies" is an independent clause.

CONNECT THE DOTS

PUNCTUATION PRACTICE:

Look in the glossary for a list of conjunctions. Then choose the one that would best connect the following:

We are out of chips; I'm hungry for chips and salsa.

A: We are out of chips, but I'm hungry for chips and salsa.

COMPOUNDING
RESULTS

*T*he name for a sentence with two independent clauses is "compound." Certain words and phrases often join those clauses: *nevertheless, therefore, otherwise, however, finally, eventually, certainly, as a result, consequently.*

When a semicolon separates a compound sentence, the connecting word (or words) is followed by a comma.

Marcia does not like seafood; therefore, we should not cook shrimp.

The connecting words shown on page 21 are adverbs. They describe how, when, or for what reason something is done. That is why they are used as linking words!

PUNCTUATION PRACTICE:

Where would the punctuation marks go in the following compound sentences?

Josie made a sandwich as a result she was no longer hungry

Take the seeds out of the pepper otherwise it might be too spicy

A: Take the seeds out of the pepper, otherwise,
it might be too spicy!

INGREDIENTS
FOR
SUCCESS

Colons and semicolons can be helpful ingredients as you create sentences. Sometimes you need to make a list or use an example.

Other times, you want to show how closely two thoughts are tied together. Keep practicing with punctuation, and your writing will always be a treat!

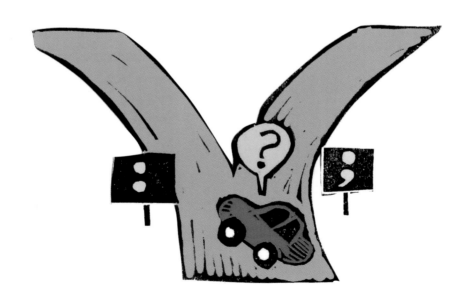

-ACTIVITY-

COMPLETE
THE
THOUGHT

Use the punctuation clues in the left-hand column to find the rest of the sentence. Are you looking for a list, a connecting word, or another independent clause? Copy the words in the columns at right onto your own sheet of paper. Then rearrange them to get the correct combinations.

The cupcake had too much frosting;	it burned.
Please use these toppings:	nevertheless, I licked it off.
I forgot the pie in the oven;	M&Ms, sprinkles, and brownie bits.

GLOSSARY

clause: a unit that makes up a sentence

coordinating conjunction: one of the words (*for, and, nor, but, or, yet, so*) that connects clauses

sentences: groups of words that have a noun as the subject and a verb

subject: the noun that is what or whom the sentence is about

verb: an action or state of being needed to complete a sentence

READ MORE

Bruno, Elsa Knight. *Punctuation Celebration*. New York: Henry Holt, 2009.

Pulver, Robin. *Punctuation Takes a Vacation*. New York: Holiday House, 2003.

WEBSITE

Grammar Blast

http://www.eduplace.com/kids/hme/k_5/grammar/

Test yourself on what you know about sentences and other punctuation.

Note: Every effort has been made to ensure that the website listed above is suitable for children, that it has educational value, and that it contains no inappropriate material. However, because of the nature of the Internet, it is impossible to guarantee that sites will remain active indefinitely or that their contents will not be altered.

INDEX